BODY SYSTEMS

The Digestive System

by Kay Manolis

Consultant:
Molly Martin, M.D.
Internal Medicine
MeritCare, Bemidji, MN

D1404091

BLASTOFF! 4 READERS

BELLWETHER MEDIA · MINNEAPOLIS, MN

Note to Librarians, Teachers, and Parents:

Blastoff! Readers are carefully developed by literacy experts and combine standards-based content with developmentally appropriate text.

Level 1 provides the most support through repetition of high-frequency words, light text, predictable sentence patterns, and strong visual support.

Level 2 offers early readers a bit more challenge through varied simple sentences, increased text load, and less repetition of high-frequency words.

Level 3 advances early-fluent readers toward fluency through increased text and concept load, less reliance on visuals, longer sentences, and more literary language.

Level 4 builds reading stamina by providing more text per page, increased use of punctuation, greater variation in sentence patterns, and increasingly challenging vocabulary.

Level 5 encourages children to move from "learning to read" to "reading to learn" by providing even more text, varied writing styles, and less familiar topics.

Whichever book is right for your reader, Blastoff! Readers are the perfect books to build confidence and encourage a love of reading that will last a lifetime!

This edition first published in 2016 by Bellwether Media, Inc.

Library of Congress Cataloging-in-Publication Data
Manolis, Kay.
  Digestive system / by Kay Manolis.
     p. cm. – (Blastoff! readers: body systems)
  Includes bibliographical references and index.
  Summary: "Introductory text explains the functions and physical concepts of the digestive system with color photography and simple scientific diagrams. Intended for students in grades three through six"–Provided by publisher.
  ISBN: 978-1-60014-243-7 (hardcover : alk. paper)
  ISBN: 978-1-62617-470-2 (paperback : alk. paper)
  1. Digestive organs–Juvenile literature. I. Title.

  QP145.M363 2009
  612.3–dc22   2008032699

Contents

What Is the Digestive System?

It's time for lunch! Food contains **nutrients** that give you energy, help you grow, and keep you alive. Your digestive system breaks down food so that the nutrients can be used by your body.

Nutrients

Different kinds of food have different nutrients. Fruits and vegetables are high in **vitamins**. Meats, eggs, and nuts have a lot of **protein**. Bread, cereal, and fruits are full of **carbohydrates**.

Your body must break down food into very tiny parts in order to get these nutrients. This is the job of the digestive system.

fun fact

Most solid foods take about 24 hours to move through the whole digestive system.

Parts of the Digestive System

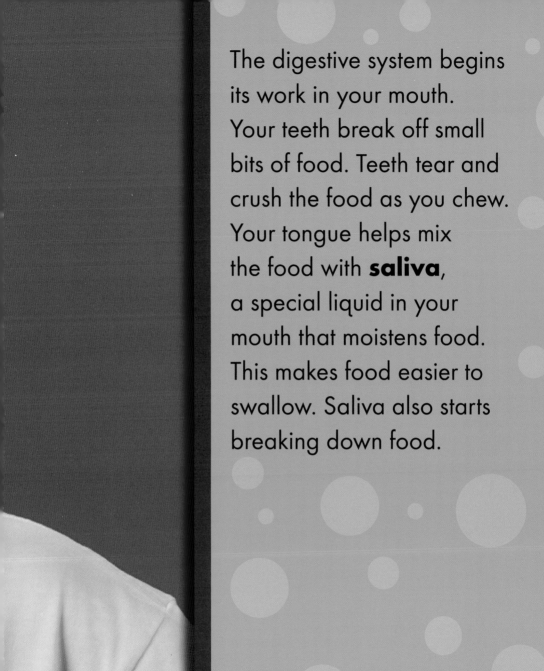

The digestive system begins its work in your mouth. Your teeth break off small bits of food. Teeth tear and crush the food as you chew. Your tongue helps mix the food with **saliva**, a special liquid in your mouth that moistens food. This makes food easier to swallow. Saliva also starts breaking down food.

When you swallow, food moves into a tube called the **esophagus**. Its walls are made of muscles. They squeeze to push food down the esophagus. These muscles work automatically whenever food is present. This means your brain makes them work without you thinking about it.

! fun fact

The muscles in your esophagus work so well that they could push food into your stomach even if you were standing on your head.

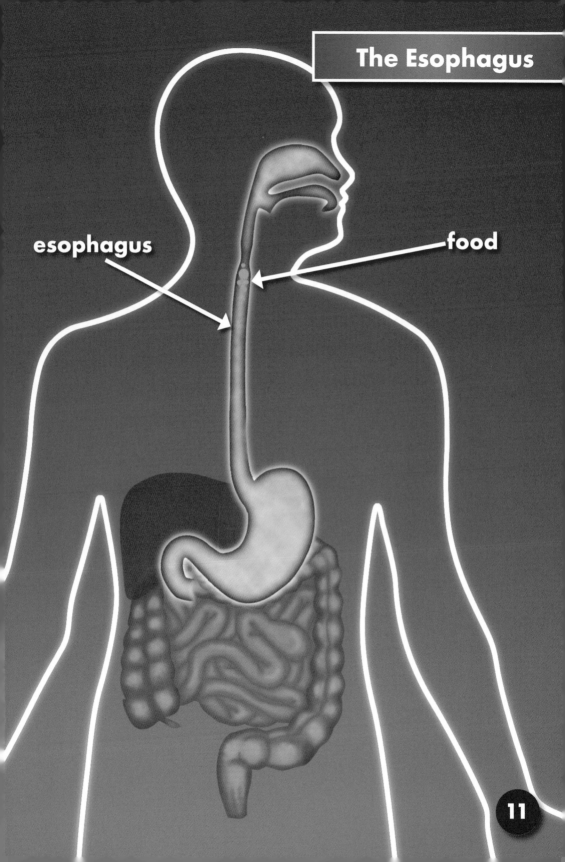

esophagus

food

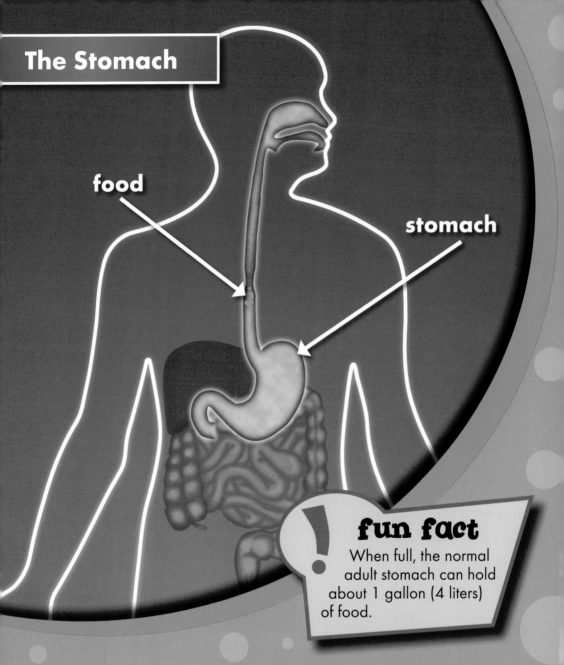

food

stomach

fun fact

When full, the normal adult stomach can hold about 1 gallon (4 liters) of food.

Food moves from the esophagus into the **stomach**. The stomach is like a small bag that can stretch to hold the food you swallow.

The walls of the stomach are made of powerful muscles. These squeeze to mash up food even more. **Acids** and other liquids in the stomach continue the job of breaking down food. Acids also kill **germs** in food that could make you sick.

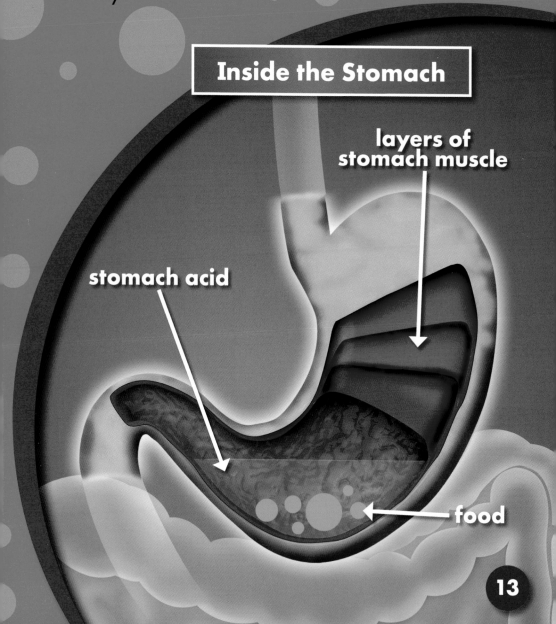

Inside the Stomach

layers of
stomach muscle

stomach acid

food

Solid food stays in the stomach for one to four hours. By the end of this time, it is turned into a thick, liquid mixture. This food mixture passes from the stomach into a tube called the **small intestine**. This tube twists and turns to fit into a small space underneath your stomach. The small intestine breaks down the food even more.

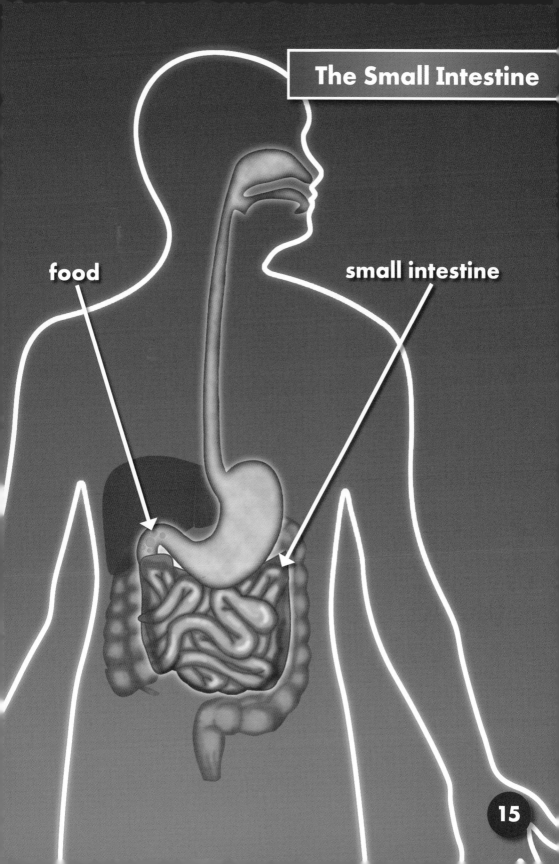

food

small intestine

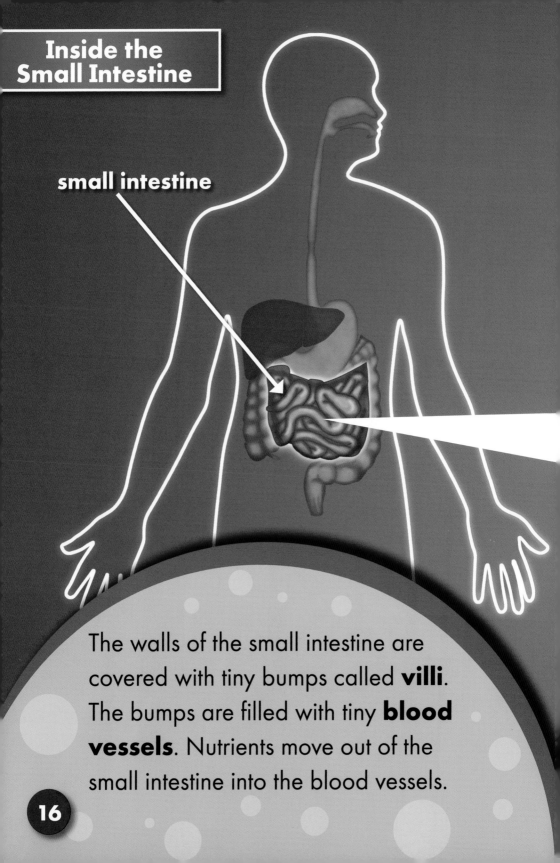

small intestine

The walls of the small intestine are covered with tiny bumps called **villi**. The bumps are filled with tiny **blood vessels**. Nutrients move out of the small intestine into the blood vessels.

Blood carries the nutrients to **cells** in every part of your body. There, the nutrients can be used to give your body energy.

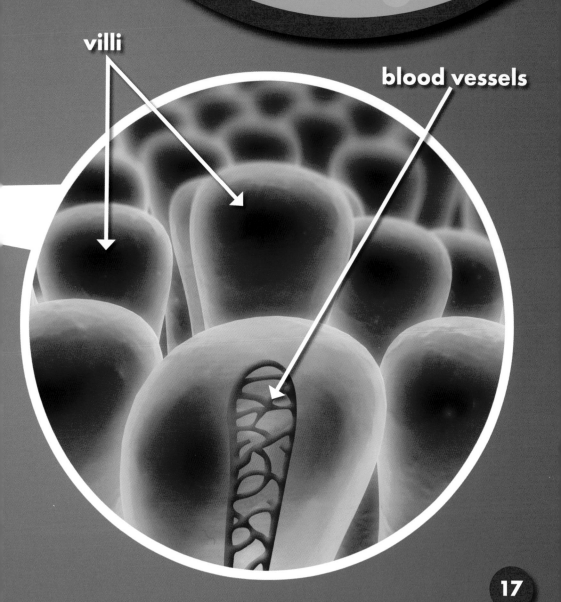

villi

blood vessels

large intestine

Your body can't use all the parts of the food you eat. Some of it becomes waste. The waste material moves into the **large intestine**. This runs under and along the sides of the small intestine. The large intestine is shorter than the small intestine. It is called "large" because it is much thicker.

Your body soaks up water from waste material in the large intestine. This makes the material become solid again. Eventually, the solid waste leaves the body when you go to the bathroom.

Staying Healthy

Your body needs a balance of nutrients to function at its best. The best way to get this balance is to eat a variety of healthy foods every day.

Exercise is also important for staying healthy. Have fun using the energy you get from your food!

Glossary

acids—sour substances; acids break down foods into their basic nutrients.

blood vessels—strong tubes that carry blood throughout the body

carbohydrates—nutrients found in foods such as bread, cereal, and fruits

cells—the basic building blocks of living things

esophagus—the tube that carries food and liquid from the mouth to the stomach

germs—tiny living things; many germs can cause illness in people.

large intestine—the tube after the small intestine; food waste moves through the large intestine and passes out of the body.

nutrients—substances that are necessary for living things to stay alive and healthy

protein—a nutrient; proteins are the building blocks of bones, muscles, skin, and blood.

saliva—a liquid inside your mouth; saliva begins the process of breaking down food.

small intestine—the tube that runs between the stomach and large intestine; most nutrients from food are absorbed in the small intestine.

stomach—the part of your digestive system where chewed food begins to be digested

villi—small bumps in the small intestine that absorb nutrients

vitamins—nutrients found in many foods, especially fruits and vegetables

To Learn More

AT THE LIBRARY

Green, Emily K. *Healthy Eating*. Minneapolis, Minn.: Bellwether, 2007.

Simon, Seymour. *Guts: Our Digestive System*. New York: HarperCollins, 2006.

Taylor-Butler, Christine. *The Digestive System*. New York: Children's Press, 2008.

ON THE WEB

Learning more about the digestive system is as easy as 1, 2, 3.

1. Go to www.factsurfer.com.

2. Enter "digestive system" into the search box.

3. Click the "Surf" button and you will see a list of related Web sites.

With factsurfer.com, finding more information is just a click away.

Index

The images in this book are reproduced through the courtesy of: Sebastian Kaulitzki, front cover, p. 17;
Monkey Business Images, pp. 4, 20; Juan Martinez, pp. 6-7; Linda Clavel, diagrams, pp. 10-11, 12, 13,
14-15, 16, 17, 18-19; Rich Legg, p. 21.